Raging dragons, leaping cows, and baseball-playing dogs all come together in this zany collection that explores a host of feelings.

"...a striking, unusual book..."
— ◆ *Kirkus Reviews*

"Children will delight in guessing each emotion and in letting their imaginations run wild as they make up stories to go with each picture."
— ★ *Parents' Choice*

"Bold, colorful graphics distinguish this picture book from the hundreds of other ABCs and books on feelings."
— *Booklist*

"...an exceptional work—colorful, original, unique."
— *School Library Journal*

"Wacky." — *Newsweek*

"One side of this jazzy, ingenious book offers a swing through the alphabet; flipped upside-down, it becomes a counting book of cavorting critters."
—*Publishers Weekly*

Woodleigh Marx Hubbard was born into a family of five children. Encouraged by her parents to be curious about the world around her, at the age of twenty, she set off on a journey around the world. She studied art at the Corcoran School of Art in Washington, D.C., the School of Visual Arts in New York, and the Academy of Beaux Arts in Paris. Ms. Hubbard currently lives in Washington. She loves creating books for children.

To Eric and Vickie whose unconditional love continuously
has a profound impact on my life. I love you.

Acknowledgements:
I'd like to thank my editor, Victoria Rock, for her unwavering support for me and this book;
Karen Pike for her excellent taste; Kendra Marcus for her clarity and wisdom; and my parents
for teaching me through their example that a vision is achievable.

Library of Congress Cataloging-in-Publication Data

Hubbard, Woodleigh.
        C is for curious / Woodleigh Hubbard.
        64p.   25.4 x 24.4cm.
        Summary: Presents an alphabet of emotions, from angry to zealous.
        ISBN 0-8118-1078-X (pb.)
        ISBN 0-87701-679-8 (hc.)
        1. Emotions—Juvenile literature. 2. Alphabet—Juvenile literature. (1. Emotions. 2. Alphabet.) I.
Title.
        BF561.H82 1990
        152.4—dc20
        (E)   90-1170
                                                                                          CIP
                                                                                          AC

Distributed in Canada by Raincoast Books
8680 Cambie Street, Vancouver, B.C. V6P 6M9

10 9 8 7 6 5 4 3

Chronicle Books
85 Second Street
San Francisco, California 94105

www.chroniclebooks.com

C IS FOR CURIOUS

AN
A B C
OF
FEELINGS

BY
WOODLEIGH
HUBBARD

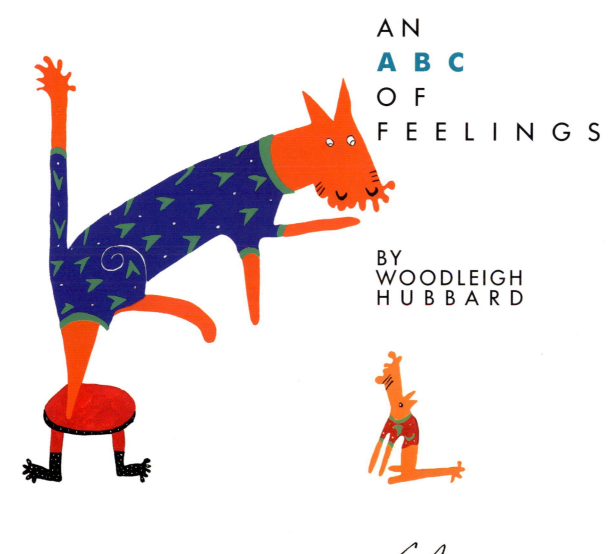

chronicle books
San Francisco

ANGRY

BORED

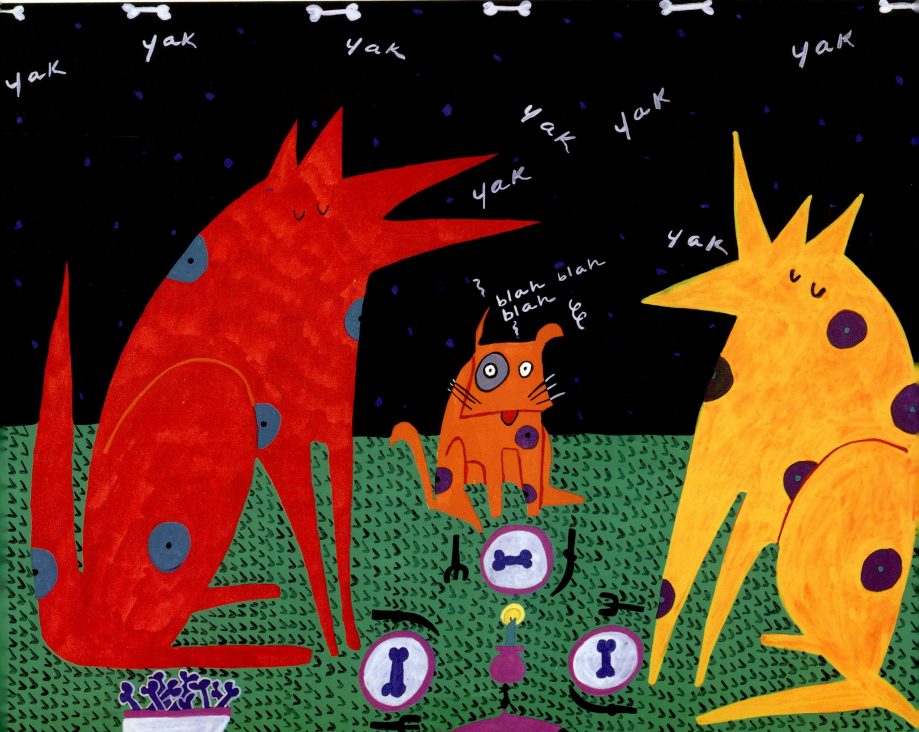

CURIOUS

DOUBTFUL

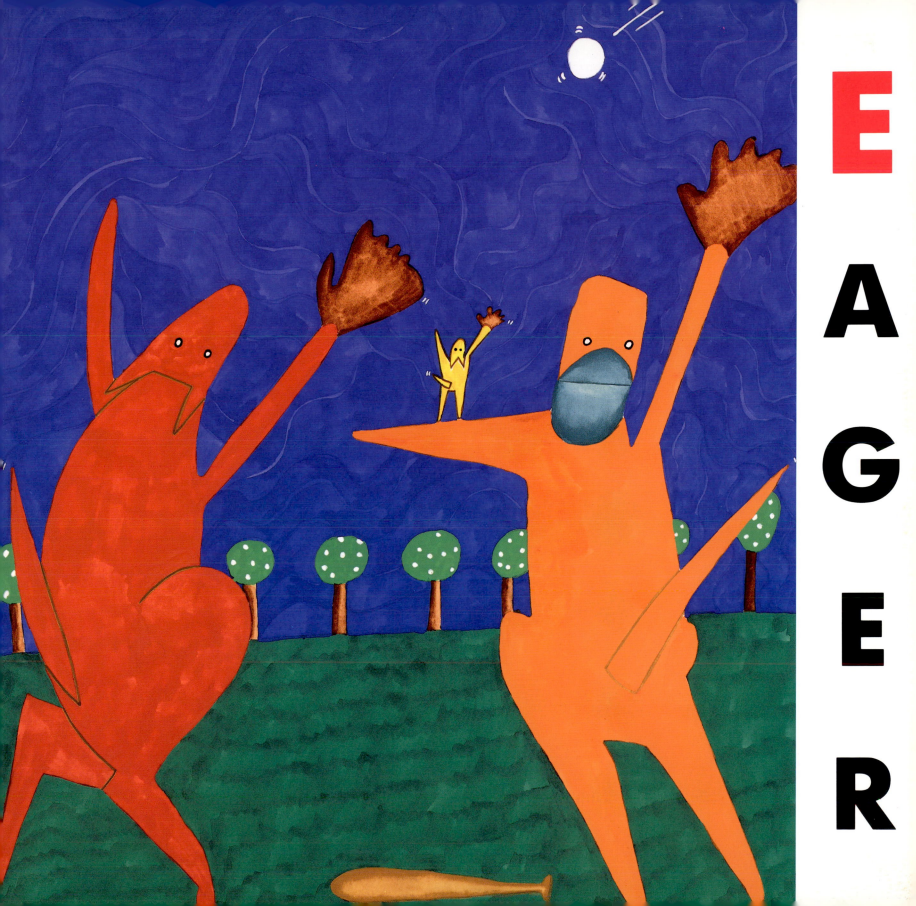

FRIGHTENED

GIGGLY

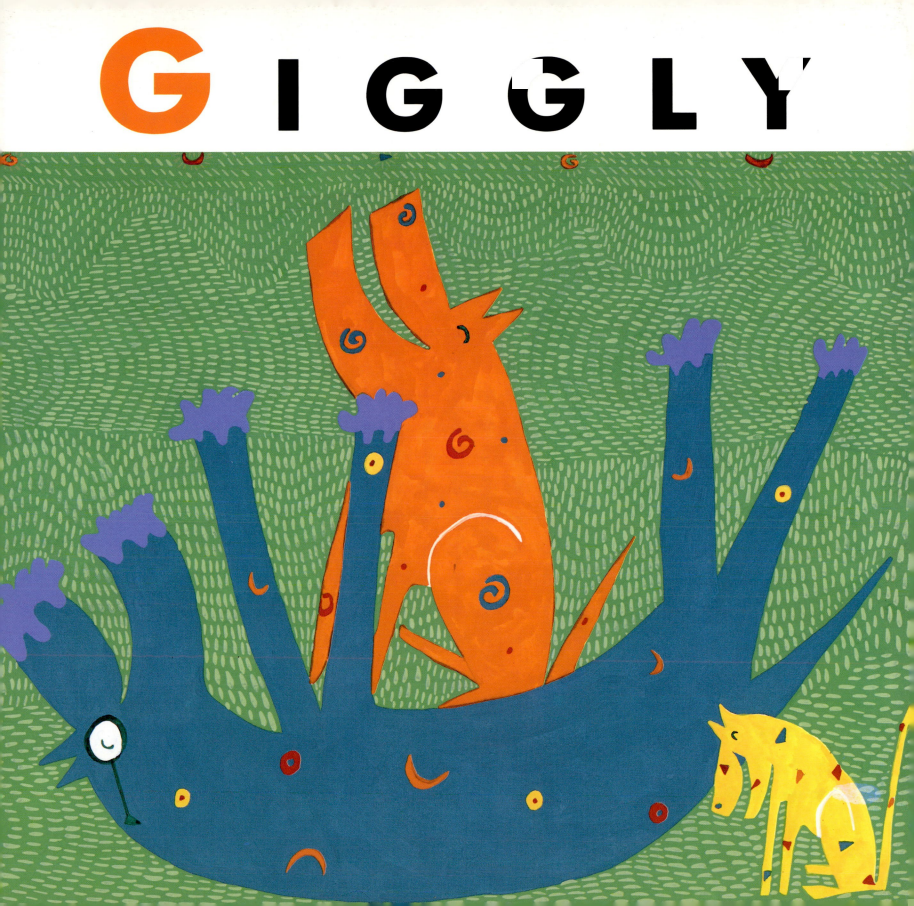

IMPATIENT

JEALOUS

K

I

N

D

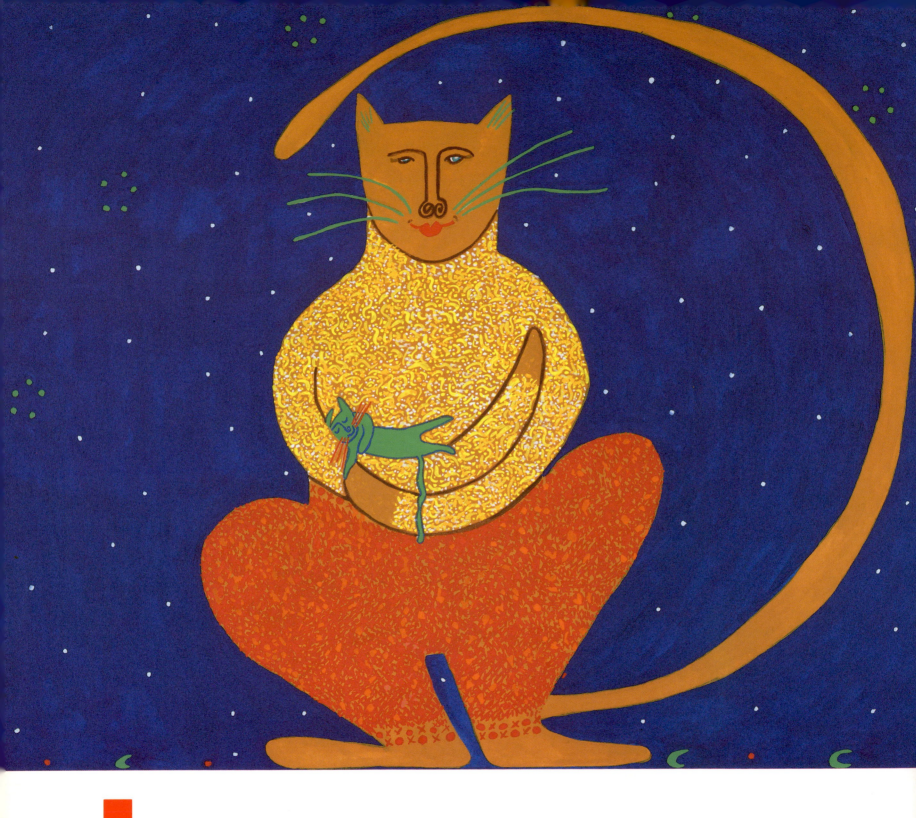

LOVING

MOODY

OBEDIENT

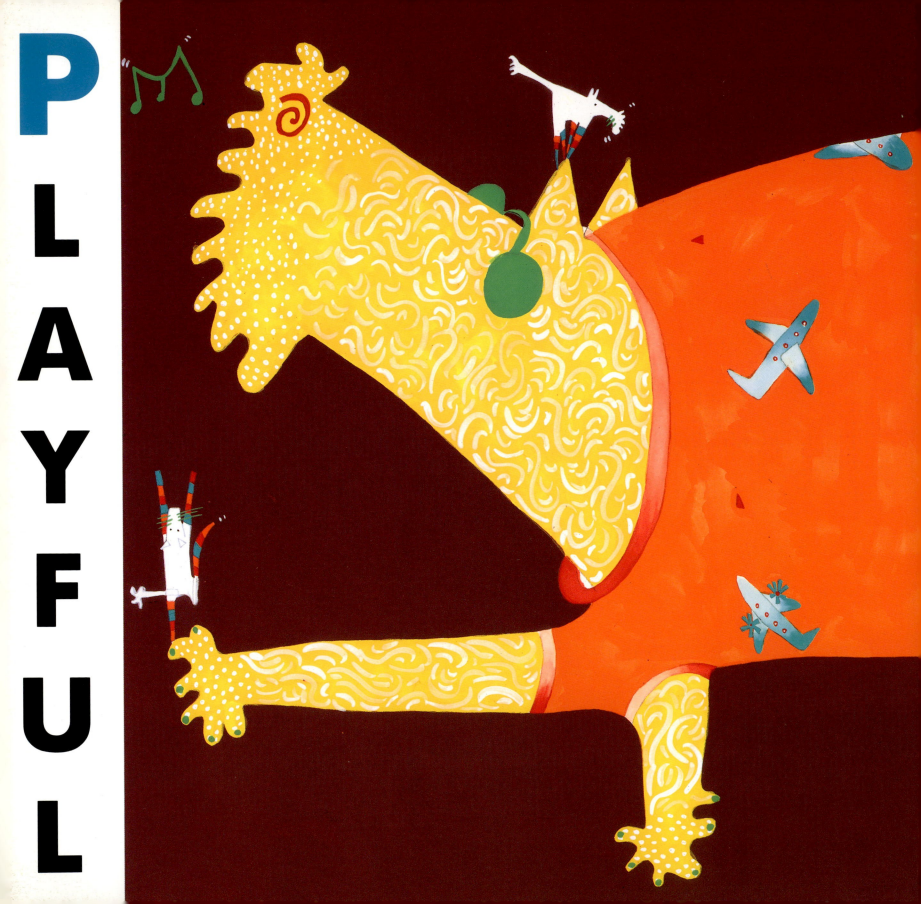

PLAYFULL

QUIET

RESTLESS

TEARFUL

UNDER

STANDING

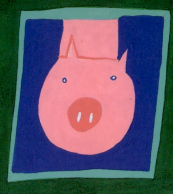

V
A
I
N

ME ME ME ME ME ME ME
ME ME ME ME ME ME ME ME
ME ME ME ME ME ME ME ME
ME ME ME ME ME ME ME
ME ME ME ME ME ME ME
ME ME ME ME ME ME ME
ME ME ME ME ME ME ME
ME ME ME ME ME ME
ME ME ME ME ME ME ME ME
ME ME ME ME ME ME ME ME
ME ME ME ME ME ME ME ME
ME ME ME ME ME ME ME ME
ME ME ME ME ME ME ME ME
ME ME ME ME ME ME ME ME
ME ME ME ME ME ME
ME ME ME ME ME

WILD

Xenophobic

YUCKY

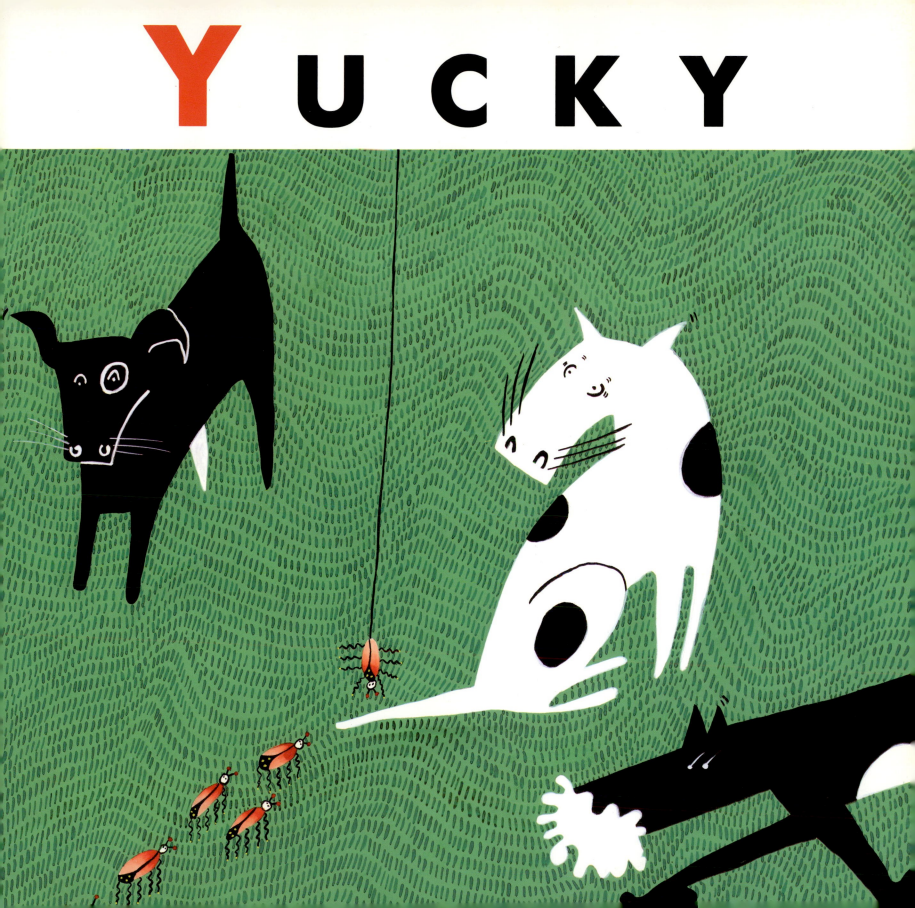

TRAVELING

CELEBRATING

9 IS FOR

RIDING

8 IS FOR

FISHING

7 IS FOR

READING

6 IS FOR

2 is for Dancing

SINGING

5 IS FOR

FLOATING

4 IS FOR

JUMPING

3 IS FOR

DANCING

2 IS FOR

DREAMING

1 IS FOR

2 IS FOR DANCING

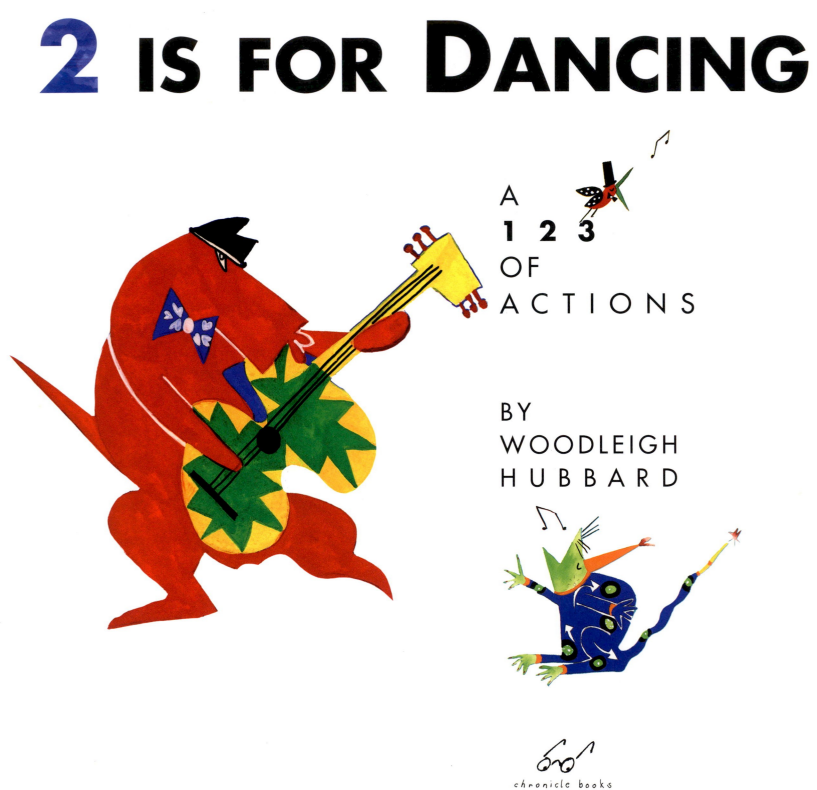

A
1 2 3
OF
ACTIONS

BY
WOODLEIGH
HUBBARD

chronicle books
San Francisco

To my sisters Suzanne and Alexandra and my brothers Wade
and Lloyd, who unfailingly bring great wit, depth, inspiration,
and love to my life!

Acknowledgements:
I'd like to thank Victoria Rock for the joy she is to work with; Jill Brubaker for her
ability to effectively accomplish so many things at one time; Kendra Marcus for her
friendship and for creating miracles; Karen Pike for being my brilliant "silent" partner;
and Thaw for her inexhaustible joy at all times!

Printed in Hong Kong.
Library of Congress Cataloging-in-Publication Data

Hubbard, Woodleigh.
    Two is for dancing : a 1 2 3 of actions / by Woodleigh Hubbard.
    64p.   25.4 x 24.4cm.
    Summary: A counting book introducing different types of actions, from one unicorn dreaming to
ten dogs riding a bicycle.
    ISBN 0-8118-1078-X (pb.)
    ISBN 0-87701-895-2 (hc.)
    (1. Counting. 2. Animals—Fiction.) I. Title. II. Title: 2 is for dancing.
    PZ7.H8624Tw   1991
    (E)—dc20   91-8076
                                                   CIP
                                                     AC

Distributed in Canada by Raincoast Books
8680 Cambie Street, Vancouver, B.C. V6P 6M9

10 9 8 7 6 5 4 3

Chronicle Books
85 Second Street
San Francisco, California 94105

www.chroniclebooks.com

One unicorn dreaming under a star-strewn sky. Six little chicks cuddled together reading. Eight energetic dogs wildly riding a bicycle. These are just some of the wacky and wonderful creatures that readers will encounter in this exuberant exploration of numbers and verbs.

"...the joyous enthusiasm in each picture is pleasantly contagious."
—*Kirkus Reviews*

"Hubbard's zany characters breathe life into the highly visual verbs she has chosen . . ."
—*Publishers Weekly*

". . . a stunning picture book."
—*School Library Journal*

". . . dazzling, imaginative. . . . A unique way to learn numbers."
—*Boston Globe*

". . . one book to count on . . ."
—*Child Magazine*

OTHER BOOKS ILLUSTRATED BY WOODLEIGH MARX HUBBARD:

The Friendship Book

Hip Cat by Jonathan London

Imaginary Menagerie by Layne Longfellow

Woodleigh Marx Hubbard's Twelve Days of Christmas